Table of Content

Introduction

How will you feel when you wake up on a Monday morning to find a message from your affiliate marketing provider in your email telling you that you have just received $1000 for a product commission you have promoted for a week? I guess you will go partying on the Friday of that week. That was exactly what I did when I made my first $1000 from affiliate marketing. That's the dream, right? To make money while you sleep. Passive income it is.

A lot of folks don't seem to understand what affiliate marketing is all about and how to get started with it. It is true you can earn 7 figures with affiliate marketing but the truth is that this can only be possible if you follow the right steps.

Affiliate marketing can be a lot of things. But as for me, it is the lazy man's technique for building wealth.

For some, it's a source of income which is unpredictable and no proofs of payments; an endless vortex of low figures and missed opportunities.

For others, it's an inspired activity that changes an addiction for analysis and a love for numbers into a viable business. And

For a few, though, it's something very special.

But as for me, affiliate marketing is more than a business:

It's a passion that governs life and makes you want to find out that special new GEO, find profit in the unthinkable places, analyze and make the best use of it like it's your last day on earth, the dream of that awesome campaign becoming profitable, sweat in nervous bouts of energy as you see a campaign that was nothing turn into something amazing.

Because this business is something different.

It's a love, a calling and a dream.

It's a struggle, an eternal fight, and a war against your own self, your fear of failure, your anxieties.

It's winning and exploring that sense of restless happiness when you make it rain.

It's more than a job.

More than a profession, steadily giving you a monthly pay cheque.

Affiliate marketing freed me from the shackles of an awfully boring, 9-to-5 job; I was released from daily torments created by overbearing bosses in claustrophobic offices.

I'm free in this competitive and super harsh world.

The idea that comes to most people's mind when you tell them you are into online businesses is either you do FOREX, or you are into some sort of cyber-crime. Only a select few people really go as far as considering the fact that there are several legitimate businesses that can be carried out on the internet.

The question now is this: what is an online business?

In my opinion, an online business is any business that is carried out on the internet. It doesn't require any physical exchange of asset or goods and services for raw cash like normal trade which is offline based.

The beauty of most online businesses is that it can be handled from virtually any place on earth as long as you have – power, internet and a capable device to stay connected on the relevant platform.

It is a career path that allows an individual to be flexible in their movement and lifestyle.

People who are interested in working for themselves rather than for an organization will be more suited to follow the online business path.

Fortunately, there are several niches in the online business industry to help interested individuals meet their financial needs, grow their portfolio and also add value to humanity.

As stated earlier, from the beginning of this book, we have online businesses of different types starting from the widely-renowned FOREX and the following listed below:

- Information Marketing
- Affiliate Marketing
- Blogging
- Freelancing

Chapter One

Why and What Is Affiliate Marketing?

Why do you want to venture into Affiliate Marketing?

Affiliate Marketing remains one of the online businesses I personally call a 'semi-automated' online business. It is semi-automated in the sense that it requires less time than other businesses to run. Once you set up the initial workflow processes, all you need do is to monitor and tweak accordingly for maximum results.

If you have a 9-5 job, you can still run Affiliate Marketing easily. You can check your dashboard and funnels when you are home in the evening or during the weekends. You don't need any special skill to start earning $$ on affiliate marketing sites. All you have to do is follow the simple step by step guide in this book, and I guarantee you that you will be smiling to the bank once you set up this business properly.

If you are work for yourself (self-employed), it is even better for you as you can commit yourself, even more, to make your results work best for you.

Now, you understand that this business is somehow self-reliant once set up properly, but what does this it really entail?

What is Affiliate Marketing?

Simply put, Affiliate Marketing refers to a marketing process where you promote products from a merchant (the affiliate company) to a targeted audience who have an interested in that product to make sales and earn commissions on each sale made.

Here is the formula below:

Affiliate product + Promotion + Target Audience = Sales = Commission (Percentage of the sale made)

This simply means that for each product you sell, you are paid a certain percentage of that sale as commission.

It is really a game of numbers and the more products you are able to sell, the better your commissions will be when you sum them up.

The commission percentage can range from 10% to as high as 100% and differs greatly based on the type of product and across different affiliate platforms as well.

So the first step in Affiliate Marketing will be to get an audience that has an interest in a product or service that you are promoting. Next is to get a product that fits their interest and then promote it to them, telling them how wonderful it is for them.

You will have to eventually pitch it to them to try it out. This is how you can make your sales and earn your commissions.

Chapter Two

Best Affiliate Marketing Platforms You Can Register On

There are several Affiliate marketing platforms you can join up for free, get their products and start promoting to your audience to earn commissions.

Most allow registrations from almost any country while others restrict some countries.

For the sake of focus, I will discuss the three best Affiliate Platforms:

- ➤ JV Zoo
- ➤ Clickbank
- ➤ Warriorplus

JV Zoo

Jvzoo focuses more on digital products and software. It is not like they don't have products on other niches, but they are quite good with their digital product offers. Most countries are legible to register under JV Zoo.

On this platform, you can receive your earnings using your Paypal and Payoneer.

Clickbank

Clickbank focuses on a wide variety of products, both physical and digital. Some countries are not allowed to register on the Clickbank platform.

On this platform, you can receive your earnings using Payoneer.

Warriorplus

Warriorplus is another very good affiliate platform. Digital products are mostly sold on this platform as well, and you can register from almost any country.

The Warriorplus platform is really newbie-friendly, and you can actually find your footing real quick.

Payments are processed through a number of means including PayPal too.

However, it is important to note that the amount of money you are likely to earn is independent of the affiliate platform you decide to go for.

Most of the popular ones are good, and commission earned is dependent on the percentage allocated to that product by the merchant.

So, feel free to register under any of the ones I have listed in this guide.

-----------Registering on ClickBank-------------

If you are registering from the countries supported by Clickbank, then go right ahead.

After registration on Clickbank, the next step is creating a Payoneer account which you will use in receiving your payments.

The registration process is self-explanatory, so go ahead and follow through then look for a tab on Payoneer showing GLOBAL PAYMENT SERVICES and click on it.

You will see that Payoneer would have created a bank account for you with your unique banking information.

Carefully, copy down this information because you will need it soon.

Carefully fill in your details on Clickbank profile page and then submit and wait a few seconds and you'll be approved that's how you register on Clickbank!

Now that we have successfully registered and gotten approved on Clickbank, the next step is
to check out the products on Clickbank to promote, search and tap on MARKETPLACE.

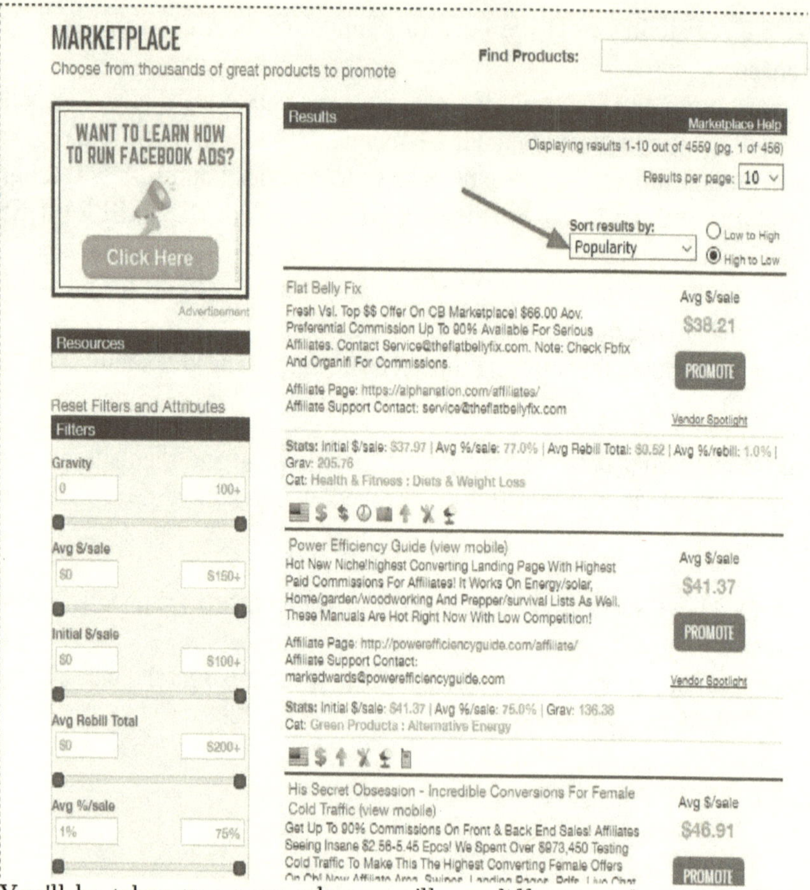

You'll be taken to a page where you'll see different niches of products that you can promote products from to earn commissions.

There are three factors to consider before you can select a product to promote.

> The price per product
> The commission percentage of the product
> The gravity of the product

I'm certain you know what the first two mean, but I'll explain the third.

The gravity of a product is a measure of the degree or volume of sales occurring on a product.

It runs from 1 - 100 or more.

The higher it is, the higher the competition to make a sale with that product because it means a lot of people are rushing to promote the product.

If it's too low, it means it's not converting well enough and has few people promoting it. Such products should be avoided if possible.
I'll personally advise you go for products with an average gravity, say between 40-50 percentage
This way, you will be able to compete to sell a hot product to an interested audience without fighting in an already-crowded space.

Now you have a product, let's set up your Payment method.
Using the Payoneer account details, scroll over to SETTINGS and PAYMENT to set up your details.
Payoneer offers a physical MasterCard about a month after you register with them.

Chapter Three

Product Categories You Should Consider

If it comes to selling products offline or online, there are certain niches known as-EVERGREEN which have a certain characteristic.

Being evergreen here means the market is always hot in demand and will have a ready audience that needs products to solve their problems.

These niches are of three types:

• Health

• Wealth

• Relationship

All of them have multiple sub-categories under which products can be further narrowed down, and under each of these sub-categories, you can find a consumer audience ready to make a purchase.

For example, you will find sub-categories under Relationship niche, like:

> Divorce
> Dating
> Break-ups
> Pre-nuptials
> Getting Back Together
> Sexual Intimacy
> Courting/ Wooing
> Sex
> Marriage etc

As you can see, all of these sub-niches falls within Relationship.

These can also be further narrowed down into smaller niches where you can now sell products that can solve the issues associated with each niche.

You can find products, for example, under Divorce such as:

> How to make a clean divorce
> How to Avoid Divorce
> How to know when your partner wants a divorce etc.

I am sure you've got the hint now.

In Affiliate Marketing, you need to concentrate on each of the three above mentioned niches.

You may decide to either go with Wealth, Health or Relationship.

You can earn a good income from any of the niches as stated earlier, so it doesn't really matter which one you're going for.

NOTE: I'll encourage you to go for a niche in which you are interested in and passionate about so that your dedication can be more sustainable in the long run.

If you want to go for the Make Money Niche that is, Wealth Niche, this niche includes loads of items that appeal to the audience.

The market here applies to people who are keen to make money. Now ask yourself this question. Who doesn't want to make money?

Nobody right?

Everybody wants to make more money, and that makes this niche a very hot niche because the demand is very high, and there's a need for a solution.

People are still looking to make money.

NOTE: It is critical that you choose hot-selling products when selecting a product to promote under these three main niches. Hot-selling products are the ones which are actually on the market at the time you are joining an affiliate platform.

You just need to advertise the product to the right audience, and it will sell because the product is already enjoying a buzz on the market.

Just key in and sell the hot product just as others are doing.

You will be throwing away your resources if you want to reinvent the wheel or experiment with a product that is long forgotten and may not be as successful as it once was.

You don't want to do that so just go along with the flow as others do and make your money.

Chapter Four

Tools You Need to Become Successful in Affiliate Marketing

As any other business, to make your Affiliate Marketing journey a success, you need the right investment in resources and other necessities.

Without these devices, you may unnecessarily stumble around before you find your way, that is, if you find your way eventually.

You will need the following resources, and their functions are also included:

> Affiliate link (the web link to the affiliate sales page that you

promote)
- ➢   Traffic source (a way of moving traffic to your affiliate offers using SEO, Facebook ads or solo ad emails);
- ➢   Lead magnet (a free but useful offer to lure in subscribers. It could be in the form of an e-book or a call-to-action text)
- ➢   Page Builder (Getresponse Native builder, Thrivearchitect, or Instabuilder plugin)
- ➢   Auto-responder (MailChimp, Getresponse, or Aweber)
- ➢   Email copy (Marketing mail copies written by you or the Brand Promoter)

Below is an affiliate marketing flow chart using an email list:

Solo ads traffic-> Landing Page-> Subscribers-> (Email List + Auto-responder emails) = SALES

We are going to clarify how this process works next so

PAY RAPT ATTENTION HERE!

First, use a page builder of your choice (Getresponse native builder, Thrivearchitect or Instabuilder), to create a landing page or squeeze page.

Note that your landing page is a channel for receiving information such as emails from interested leads/subscribers through your traffic source (a solo ads vendor). I will show you where to get cool solo ads vendors later in this guide, so keep reading.

You will have to send your landing page link to the solo ads vendor who then pushes their targeted email traffic to your landing page to your offer.

This traffic consists of people who are already interested in this niche of products which you are promoting. They are typically made up of individuals in the email list of the traffic provider.

When your audience has been sent to your landing page, and their curiosity is captured, they will sign up for the deal on your landing page to find out more or download your Freebie.

You will need a Lead Magnet to make your landing page very attractive to the traffic audience.

A lead magnet is any valuable piece of item that can attract an audience to take action on your page.

For instance, your landing page might direct your traffic to their names and email to download your lead magnet, which might be a free e-book like - 'how to make money from thin air.'

I'm sure you would have come across squeeze and landing pages which offers you a free but valuable downloadable offer.

To do so, you need to type a name and email address to get it.
If you have already integrated your landing page with an email marketing platform, they will be automatically moved to your e-mail marketing system once you get signups.

The email system saves the newly received emails to create your own new email -list that you can name as you wish.
E-mail marketing systems examples include MailChimp, Getresponse, Aweber, Sendinblue etc.
They all have a simple working process, but we will be working with Getresponse since their email marketing system is affiliate-friendly.
You can employ a developer to help you design and integrate your landing page with your email service provider, or you can send me a mail, and I'll send you a video about how to do it yourself.

Chapter Five

Different Methods to Getting Traffic for Your Affiliate Products Offers

Promoting affiliate products requires several strategies to bring the products to the audience that wants it.

You'll find the three common ways to advertise your affiliate products to make sales and earn commissions in this section.

> ➤ Promotion through blogs and website creation
> ➤ E-mail marketing promotion
> ➤ Promotion via PPC (Facebook Ads)

If followed as directed, these three methods are successful, but the emphasis of this course is on promoting your affiliate offers through email marketing.

The guidelines about how to manage promotions for each form of promotion are below:

Promotion through blogs and websites

You will need to have an affiliate blog or website built for you to promote the links to your affiliate product using this approach.

The name of the affiliate website must be related to the market on which you plan to concentrate. Example: If you want to promote sexual health products, choose a name related to sexual health. Sextherapist.com, hope you get the idea now.

To get a website for your affiliate promotion, go to Fiverr.com and hire a professional web designer to design one for you, or you can send me a message to connect you to a designer who can build one for you at a low price.

First, you will need to build content on the affiliate website using specific search keywords related to your niche to boost your website rankings to pull in traffic from search engines like Google.

You'll need the following setup for yourself:

✓ Let a WordPress specialist set up an affiliate website with a SPECIFIC NICHE of affiliate products for you.

✓ Have the marketing posts and pages of your website tailored for search engine traffic ideally to be an SEO professional who leverages keywords.

- ✓ A traffic source using Google Adwords or Facebook ads when you can afford the budget

Promotion by PPC such as Facebook Advertising

This is another way to promote your link from your affiliate product to your target audience.

This includes using PPC advertising that often means pay per click and applies to leverage Facebook-targeted traffic from a particular audience that has shown interest in the product category that you are promoting.

The reality is that Facebook doesn't encourage affiliate links on their platform.

You can make use of Content Marketing if you must use Facebook.

Create an interesting, informative content relating to the product that you want to market. It should be in the form of an article or a blog post with a redirecting link to your squeeze page or affiliate website.

Do not forget to use a squeeze page to collect their emails so that you can then retarget them directly using Email marketing.

If you don't incorporate a squeeze page to collect emails, you can still redirect them to your website from the Facebook ad post, but potential subscribers would be lacking because you don't have the means to collect their contact details.

Instead, if you have a customer opt-in form with a freebie to draw them in, you can always drive it to your website.

Any way you want to go about it, if done correctly you can be sure it works well.

In order to promote your affiliate product links using Facebook, you will need the following:

- ✓ Interesting and/or informative post regarding the products you want to promote on Facebook
- ✓ Targeted Facebook ad using your informative post
- ✓ Link to your affiliate product squeeze page or link to your affiliate website link where you can harvest their e-mails for marketing purposes.

Chapter six

Affiliate Marketing Using Email platform

This is the soul of this Affiliate Marketing guide, so be attentive here.

You need the following in the following order to promote affiliate products using the email lists:

- Landing Page
- Web Traffic Source for emails
- Email marketing platform
- Email Sales Copy

Here's how to set up your first marketing campaign for your affiliates product.

Landing page

First, to be able to launch WordPress and install a landing page builder, you must have a domain name and hosting.

Your website's name should be the name of your domain which should be either generic or related to the niche you have interest in.

It typically goes together for about $10 a year for both of them. For your domain and hosting, you can go to Namecheap, or use any other web hosting service of your choice.

You will have to install WordPress on it once your domain name goes live to enable you to view it properly on a web browser.

To do this, use your web hosting login information which will be sent to the email inbox you used to register on Namecheap to login to your C-panel, scroll to your File Manager then click on it, scroll to Softaculous and click it.

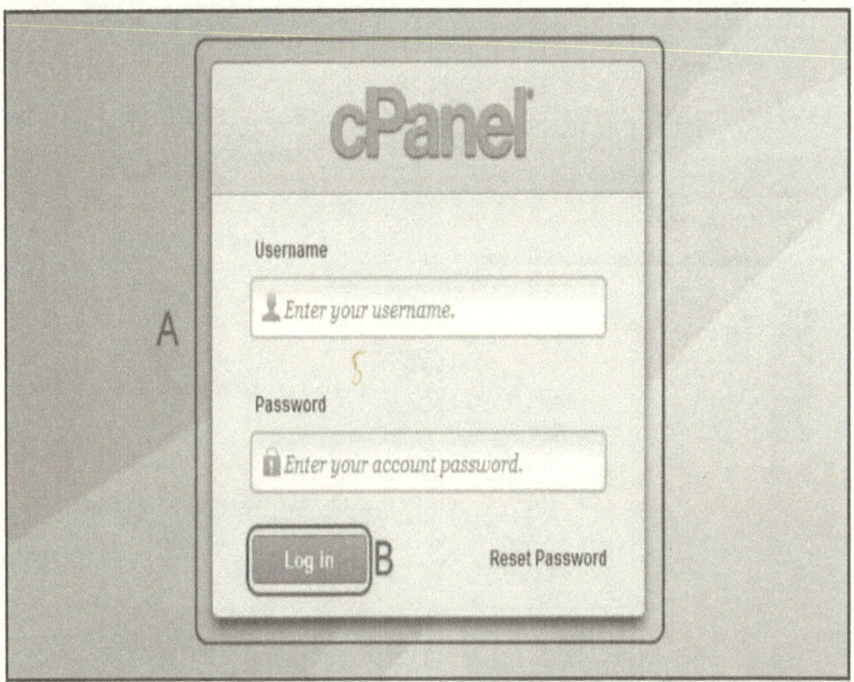

To install it, you will be redirected to a page where you need to click on the WordPress icon, choose a username and password plus other details. The next step after you have installed WordPress is to visit your website by typing it in your browser's search bar.

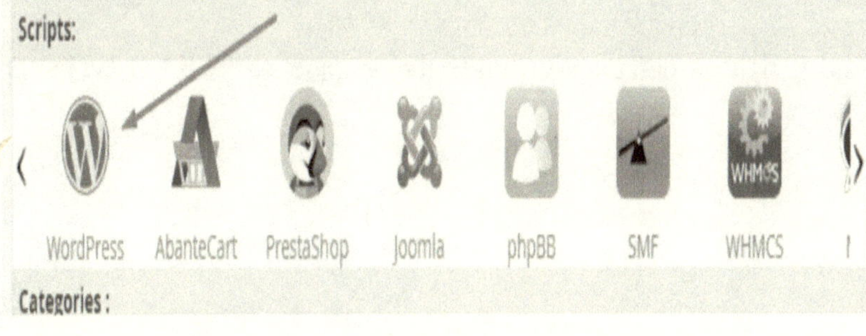

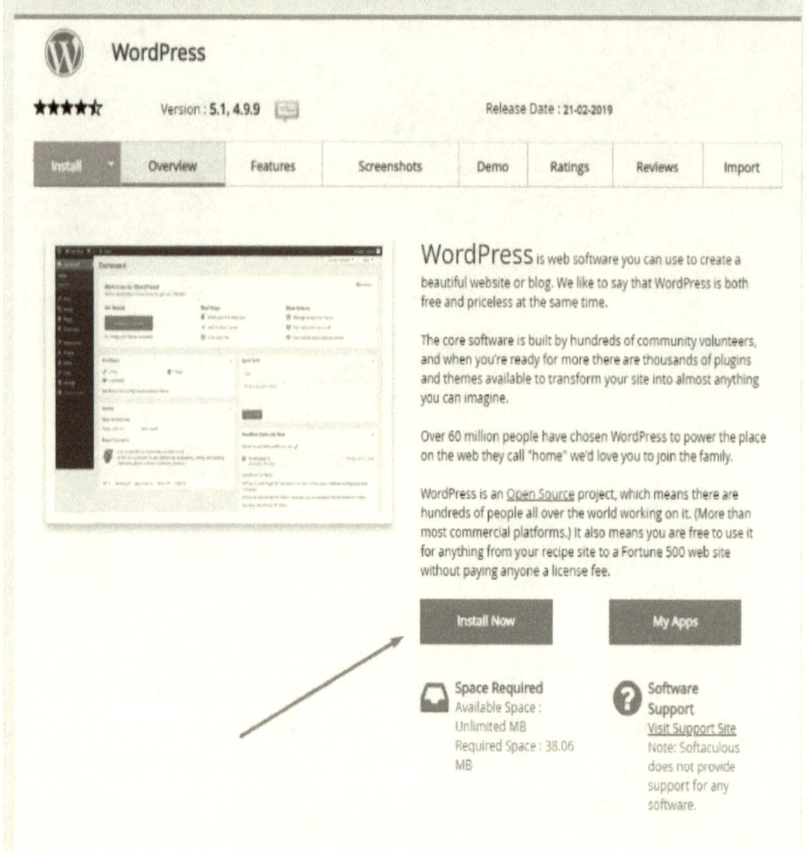

If you did it right, a default WordPress theme showing 'HELLO WORLD' will show up.

My blog

Just another WordPress site

Hello world!

Welcome to WordPress. This is your first post. Edit or delete it, then start blogging!

December 18, 2014   1 Comment

Proudly powered by WordPress

You'll also have a dashboard with a WordPress login link like this domainname.com/wp-login.php.

NOTE: WordPress is one of the content management systems used to manage a website's content.

Next, to create the first squeeze page or landing page, you will need to install a website builder plugin on the WordPress Dashboard.

To do that, if you don't have it, you might need to visit the Thrivearchitect or Instabuilder website to buy their plugin. You can shoot me a mail to forward Instabuilder plugin to you.

I am using the plugin Instabuilder for this guide.

Installing:

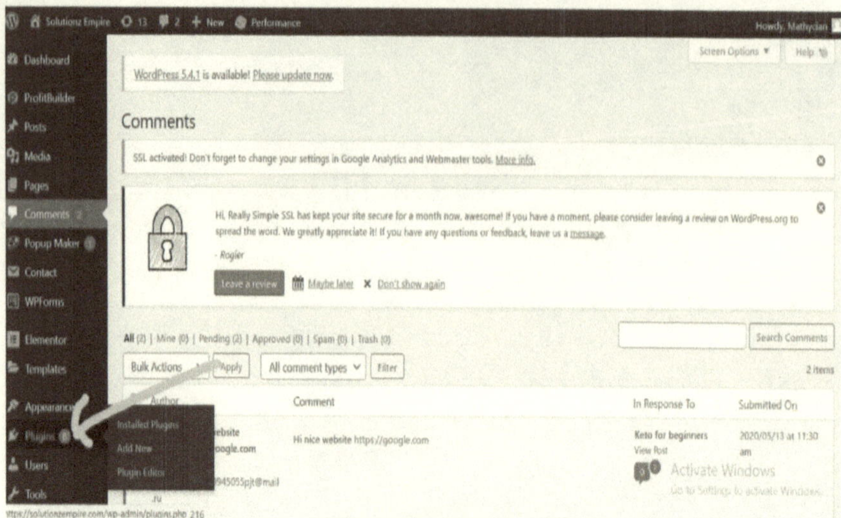

Scroll to Plugins from your WP dashboard (WP is short for WordPress), click on it then go to Add new then Upload plugin to load and install the page builder plugin.

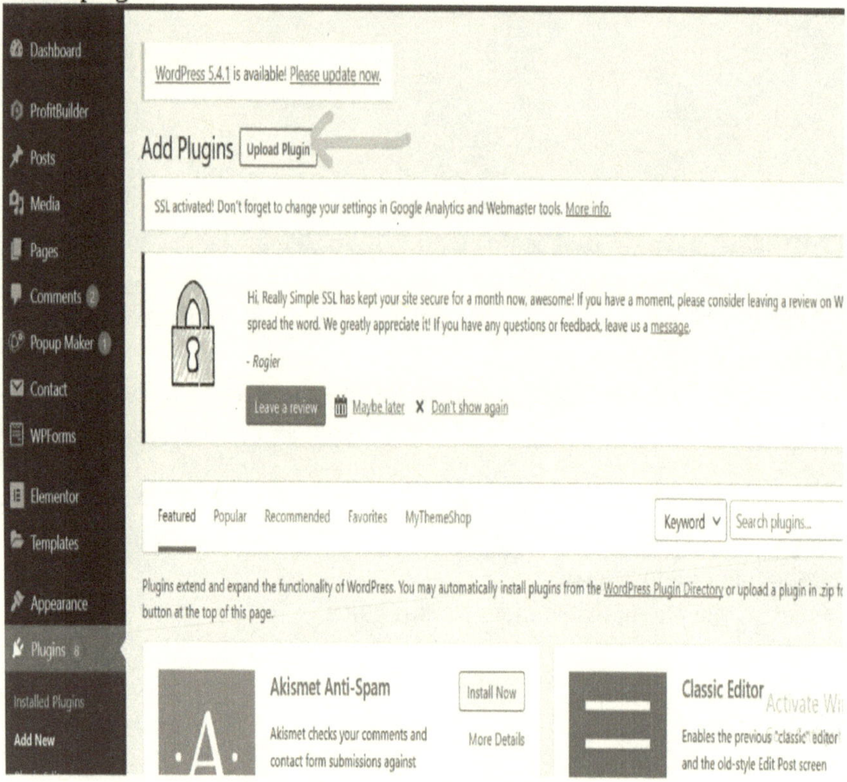

Activate it and go to your dashboard. Select Create a page to create a landing or squeeze page, and check the next page that opens.

You'll notice several different templates from which you can choose to build your landing or squeeze page.

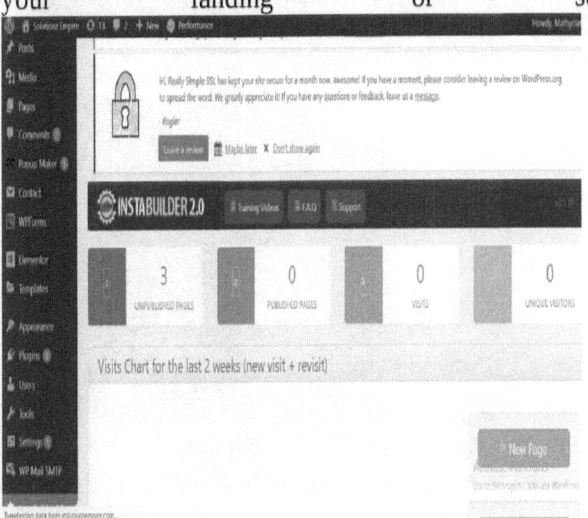

The choice is yours, so choose a template that fits the squeeze page design features that you have in mind.

You'll need to customize it accordingly after picking a template to fit your lead magnet offering.

A professional squeeze page should have the elements below to make it appealing to your audience.

• Captivating Headline
• A Video or Bold and Attractive Image
• Content describing the Squeeze page
• Call to action text inviting visitors to submit their name and email to receive their free offer.
• An opt-in form to include name, email and/or telephone number.
• A lead magnet or a valuable information offer in exchange for a telephone number or an email.

Following the template already in place, make sure your squeeze page has almost all the features or elements mentioned above.

This will look a little bit like your landing page.

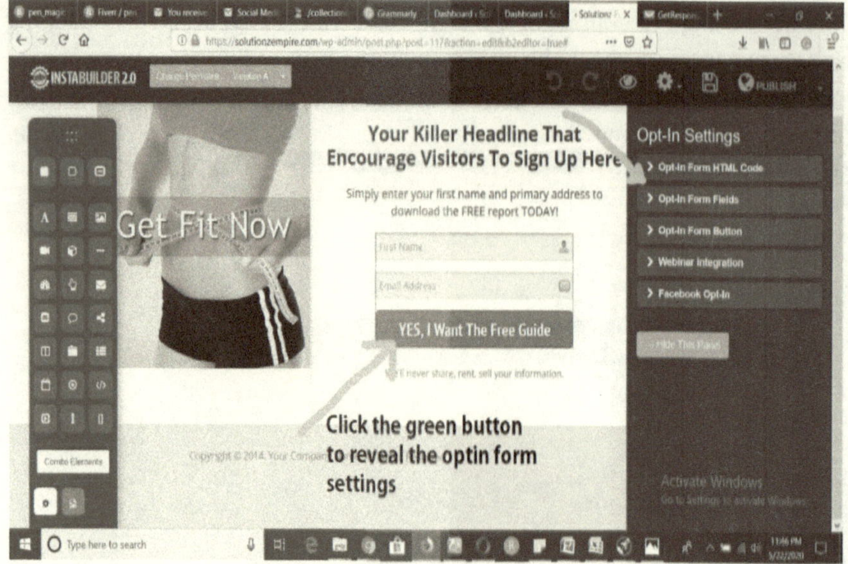

Next, you need an email marketing system like Getresponse to integrate it. Just visit the Getresponse website and then register an account to enjoy a one-month free subscription.

You need to integrate this with your new landing page after you open an account with Getresponse.

Click on Optin form settings on your Instabuilder page, and you will see a space for inputting HTML form code.

Head back to Getresponse, create a list by selecting the Getresponse dashboard and the Contacts section.

Choose a name that you can easily remember for your list and then go over to Form and Survey to create a form.

Select List Builder Wizard, select a template for the form and then create your form and save it before publishing.

Copy the form code created there and return to the opt-in form setting in Instabuilder to input this code in the HTML form code space.

To launch your landing page, click Save and Publish.

Your landing page will automatically go live, and anyone who signs into it will have their name and email sent to the list you just created on Getresponse.

If you have a Freebie or lead magnet included in your offer, there is a space provided for you to insert the lead magnet URL.

Cloud storage such as Google Drive, Dropbox, Mega or even your Web Hosting storage can create a URL for your lead magnet or freebie.

Copy the shareable link after uploading the lead magnet or freebie and paste in the space provided for it. That is on your Getresponse opt-in form settings, and you can then input this URL into the redirection URL requested for. This URL is where you want to take your subscribers to after you sign in to your offer.

Chapter seven

Traffic Source for Your Landing Page

Your next concern after you have set up and designed your landing page is TRAFFIC.

You're going to need a secure source of targeted email traffic that you send to your landing page.

Follow the link below to get registered on and make a purchase of any particular niche of your choice for targeted email traffic. https://udimi.com

The email traffic from the link above is HIGHLY TARGETED, so you have my support to go ahead and buy your solo ad emails from there.

So get the URL link to your landing page and visit the page above, buy any chosen email list number.

Price typically ranges from:

100 email traffic $35- $70

200 email traffic $70 - $140

400 email traffic $150- $250

...and so on

There are numerous bundles so you can buy as you can afford.

Once you purchase, your order will be replied by the email traffic vendor telling you when he/she will send the email traffic to your squeeze page or landing page.

When he /she has done this, you can expect people from the traffic sent to your landing page to sign up on your list.

By this time, you are expected to have email copies already offering valuable items or promoting the affiliate product on standby and scheduled to be sent daily to your new subscribers.

Email Marketing Platform

I strongly advise the use of Getresponse if you are seriously interested in using the E-mail list method to do affiliate marketing.

Compared to MailChimp, Getresponse is more lenient on affiliate promotions. So go on to GetResponse and open a new account if you haven't done so already.

The first month is free, and up to 1000 subscribers can be registered here. Afterwards, you pay $15 a month.
MailChimp is still free for only 2000 users, but they are strict, and if you do affiliate promotions, your account will be blocked without hesitation.
Click on Email Marketing and next, click on Autoresponders to start setting up your automated email sequences to promote your affiliate offers after registering with Getresponse, head over to your dashboard.
Then click Create New Autoresponder, type in Subject Line and a short message body to talk about what you're promoting and then include your affiliate link as a call to action button to check it out or get it.

Next, you need to set the date and time you want that message to go out. This is the automated email marketing feature ... that's why it's called an autoresponder.
It sends out emails after the user has set it up to follow some particular actions.
You will need to create a specific list for that autoresponder, so create a list, select a name of your choice and apply it to the autoresponder.
All mails contained in your autoresponder will go to people who join or are on that list.
You can also add more messages to your list of autoresponders, ranging from Day 0 (the day your first email is sent) to any number of Days you want.

I tend to use the format below to do 14 days for affiliate product promotion:
Day 1-Day 2 = > Send out twice a day
Day3-Day5 = > Offer Value
Day 6-Day 7 = > Send out twice a day.
Day 8-The 10th day = > No mails
Day 11-Day 12 = > Promoting twice daily with a sense of urgency like the closing of a discount.
Day 13 = > A single mail
Day 14 = > Conclude

You shouldn't follow the routine explicitly. You should find different ways of looking at what works best for you.
If you do want to follow my lead, however, please go-ahead to set up your autoresponders and other emails about automation.

Chapter 8

Pitfalls To Avoid As an Affiliate Marketer

There are a number of guidelines you have to follow if you want to succeed as an affiliate marketer. Failure to do so means that particularly if you are inexperienced in internet marketing, you won't have much success.

Follow this rules carefully and apply them:

1. Not concentrating on a niche.

Concentrate on a niche, gain experience and become an expert before switching to another niche. Stay away from switching from one audience to another.

2. Promoting various Offers at once

It sounds tempting, but it pays better to focus first of all on one product before moving to another product for promotion.

Promoting several items at once will spread your resources thinly, and can even cause confusion to the audience. At most, promote two products at a time.

3. Picking a Cold Niche

Some niches are not highly demanded, and perhaps seasonal. It is crucial that you go for evergreen niches, which are always in demand. The best niches are health, Relationship, and wealth.

4. Have a bad Landing Page

The best design on a landing page should be clean and easy to see what's on it. To set it up, you can use a pre-existing template, or find a WordPress expert to set it up for you. Nothing is to it.

5. Not collecting Emails

It would be truly terrible, as an affiliate marketer, not to receive email signups. This will happen when you run traffic directly to your sales page with no opt-in form on it.

Email marketing is a core part of affiliate marketing and should not be ignored if you really want to succeed for any reason.

6. Doing neither research nor analysis

To make affiliate marketing work for you, comprehensive market research and analysis are highly required.

You'll need to test trends, test what's happening on the market and the kind of items that customers want.

You can track product release date and search for top-selling products on your dashboard too.